ROCKET AROUND *Germany!*
A neurodiverse-friendly storybook

Written by
**Lee
Lynch**

Illustrations
**Emma
Lynch**

Contributors
**Jeffrey,
Jack, &
Tom
Lynch**

ROCKET
AROUND
LLC

This book is for neurodiverse and neurotypical kids around the world of any age, who love adventure, imagination, and finding new ways to have fun!

Neurodiverse people behave, think, and learn differently from people with neurotypical brains. These differences include strengths. In a word, neurodiverse people are awesome. Neurodiverse people might be autistic, live with ADHD, dyslexia, PTSD, Tourette's, or other things.

Safety Tips

Being safe when you travel is important. Remember to:

-Stay near the adult you are with
-Set a place to meet in case you cannot find your adult
-Know their phone number - write it here:_____
-If you feel lost, ask a police officer or information desk for help
-If your family has an emergency when in Germany, call phone number 112 (that's like 911 in the U.S.)

BE SAFE!

Everywhere We Go in This Book...

You can also see where all of the sites on this page and the next are located on the maps on Pg. 46 and 47

Everywhere We Go continued

See page 50 to be a ROCKETAROUNDER!

Hello human friend - Willkommen! (That means "Welcome" in German – see more German words on page 48) My human family is on a train going to Germany, where people speak German.

I thought after we got on the train in Switzerland, we were heading home, but a sign outside the window said, "Welcome to Germany"!

You remember my human family – Mom, Dad, Jeffrey, Jack, and Emma. We love to travel and see new things.

Sometimes they take me on their adventures. But sometimes they forget, and I have to catch them on the road, like this time.

Germany and Switzerland are located right next to each other.

About Germany

- Official name:Federal Republic of Germany
- Official language:German
- Official dog:Great Dane
- Number of cities and towns:More than 2,000
- Number of people: More than 82 million
- Located in Western Europe
- Surrounded by nine other countries: France, Luxembourg, Denmark, Belgium, Switzerland, Austria, Czech Republic, the Netherlands, and Poland

Germany is so interesting!

Munich Train Station

Germany is an old place.

Humans moved here 10,000 years ago.

The country has everything - forests, mountains, big cities, small towns, villages, and many rivers, like the Danube - one of the longest rivers in Europe.

It looks like the train has pulled into the city of Munich.

Munich is the capital of the German state Bavaria.

The largest fair in the world takes place in Munich every October.

It's called Oktoberfest, and about six million people from all over the world visit Munich for it each year.

Cool, I've always wanted to visit there!

Let's rocket around Munich together!

About Bavaria:

- Germany has 16 states.
- Bavaria is the largest state in Germany
- Bavaria is bordered by two other countries: the Czech Republic and Austria.

My family is getting off at the **Munich Train Station** ("**Hauptbahnhof**" in German).

It's one of the busiest train stations – more than 450,000 passengers come through here every day.

I wonder where they will go first? And of course we'll have to follow close behind to keep them safe.

They're walking toward **Old Town** ("**Altstadt**" in German) – Munich's historic center. So much to see here – let's go!

Old Town

Karl's Square

There are many squares here, with historic buildings, statues, and monuments connected by very old streets – some are 900 years old!

Right now, my humans are walking into **Karl's Square**. **Karl's Gate ("**Karlstor" in German) is the archway that leads into the square and is the gate to a wall that was built 800 years ago to protect the city from invaders.

Everything in Old Town is close together.

St. Michael's Church (Michaelskirche in German) is right down the street from Karlstor. "Kirche" means "church" in German.

It's one of the largest Renaissance churches – an old Roman-style church built about 600 years ago – north of the Alps mountain range.

Inside St. Michael's is the tomb of Duke Wilhelm V, who built it, and King Ludwig II, whose nickname is the "Mad King" of Bavaria.

St. Michael's Church

As we follow my humans out of the church, we can see the domed towers of the famous **Frauenkirche** (the German name for the Cathedral of Our Lady).

The people who live here tell a story that the devil left a footprint near the entrance when he thought the church had no windows.

It's not true, but it is a good story!

Frauenkirche

Wait, where are my humans?

Sniff sniff. Smells like they went this way, toward **Marienplatz,** Munich's main square.

This square is fun any time of year, and in the winter, you can visit the Christmas markets. The buildings here are amazing!

Old Town Hall

Look, there's the **German Altes Rathaus (Old Town Hall)** and **Neues Rathaus (New Town Hall)**

The **German Altes Rathaus (Old Town Hall)** was Munich's town hall until about 200 years ago. Now it has a toy museum inside.

The Neues Rathaus (New Town Hall) is where the city council and mayor work.

It has a 100-meter-tall tower with a deck at the top where you can see the whole city.

New Town Hall

Also inside is the Neues Rathaus - the **Rathaus-Glockenspiel** – a clock tower with life-sized mechanical figures that do performances about historical events. Now my family is going into the **Ratskeller München.**

It's a famous restaurant in the cellar of Neues Rathaus, with traditional German food and frescos (paintings in the wall). While my humans are taking pictures, let's eat Wiener schnitzel off Jeffrey's plate. It's a German pork chop recipe – delicious!

Ratskeller Munchen

Where are my humans going? Looks like they're heading out of Marienplaz to **Peterskirche (St. Peter's Church)**, the oldest church in Munich.

You can recognize it from the outside by its very tall church tower, known as "Alter Peter" (Old Peter in German). From the platform at the top, you can see across Munich and into the Alps mountains on clear days.

St. Peter's Church

My humans are on the move again, and it looks like they're heading over to Viktualienmarkt I love that area!

Viktualienmarkt is one of the best places in the city. It's a huge open-air market with hundreds of stalls where they sell everything – vegetables, meats and, my favorite – cheese!

In the middle of the market is the Maypole on which you can see carved pictures of the kinds of jobs people do in Munich, and especially at the market. Towns throughout Bavaria have maypoles like this one.

I could stay here all day and enjoy the food, people, music. Where are my humans going? They're on that bus. Grab on!

Maypole in Viktualienmarkt

18

They're getting off here, at **Odeonsplatz**, a famous square in Munich.

Parades and events have been held for hundreds of years.

It sits at the north end of Old Town Munich, and at the southern end **Ludwigstrasse Boulevard King Ludwig I** "(Strasse" means "street" in German)

This is a very busy boulevard that stretches through the city to **Siegestor**, (which means "Victory Gate"), a memorial arch, with four lions on top.

Ludwigstrasse was named after King Ludwig I, who created the boulevard about 200 years ago.

He made it long and wide to impress visitors and march parades along it.

Odeonsplatz has the **Feldherrnhalle (the Hall of Generals)** on one side of it and the **Theatinerkirche St. Kajetan** (Theatine Church) on the other. The Feldherrnhalle is a loggia, or a room with a roof and open side that is usually part of a building. It was built by King Ludwig I to honor the Bavarian Army.

I'm just going to stretch out on the cool stone floor and take a nap while my humans wander around Odeonsplatz.

Feldherrnhalle

They're getting off at the **Münchner Stadtmuseum (Municipal Museum),** the largest municipal museum in all of Germany. It has four million pieces of art and artifacts, and lots of cool exhibits spread across four very different buildings. The oldest building was built more than 500 years ago, one was a stable for horses, and another was an arsenal for military equipment. The museum shows the history, culture, and arts of Munich through exhibits and videos.

Yikes -- my family is getting back on the bus. Let's go!

Municipal Museum

Looks like they're getting off at the **National Theater (Opera House),** a beautiful building where the Bavarian State Opera and Ballet perform. The old Opera House burned down during a performance 200 years ago, but it was rebuilt into the building we see here today. I would stay here and show off my singing skills, but my humans are walking over to the **Cuvillies Theatre (Royal Residence)** where Bavarian monarchs lived and the famous music composer Mozart had his operas performed. Today it has several museums inside.

National Theatre

My humans are getting back on the bus – where are we going now? The **Hofbrauhaus –** time to have some fun! This is a beer hall known all over the world for its food and traditional German music.

It was built 400 years ago and back then was a brewery where the royal family's beer was made. Today anyone can visit.

Look at Jack with that huge soft pretzel!

Hey, there are two Dachshund puppies over there.

Hallo Freunde (that's Hello friends in German)! Let's go talk with them.

Dachshund:

- A type of dog breed from Germany.
- Means "badger dog" in German - they used to hunt badgers.
- Have the nickname "sausage dog" because of their shape.

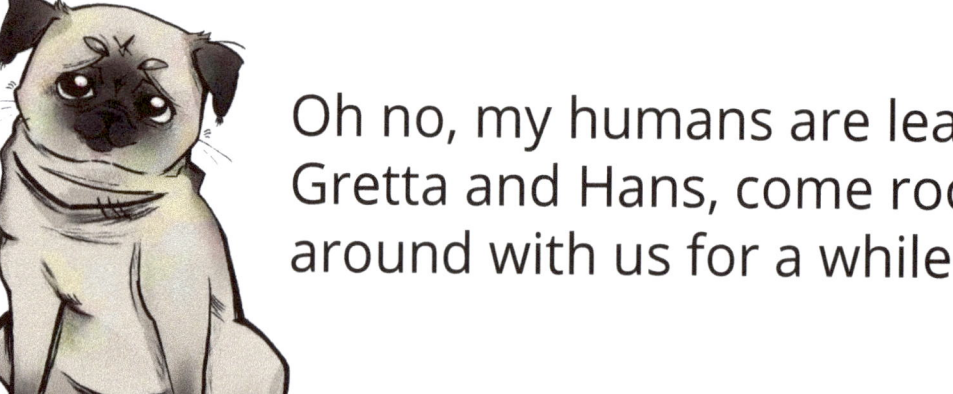

My favorite German food is Bratwurst – German sausage. Hans loves apfelstrudel – pastry with apples and spices. Try some.

When we're not working, we dance and bark with the Oompa band.

Oh no, my humans are leaving. Gretta and Hans, come rocket around with us for a while!

Now they're getting back on the bus – wonder where we are going? They're getting off at one of my favorite areas – the **Olympiastadion (Olympic Stadium) and Olympiaturm (Munich TV Tower).**

The **Olympiastadion** was built for the 1972 Summer Olympics. The roof looks like a tent and stands for openness and democracy.

You can even walk on the tent roof!

Olympic Stadium

Munich TV Tower

The Olympiastadion roof has great view, but not as incredible as the view from the top of the **Olympiaturm (Munich TV Tower) -** you can see the entire city of Munich and the Alps mountain range**.**

The Olympiaturm is almost 300 meters high (a 10-year-old human is about one and a half meters high). The Olympiaturm was the tallest building in Munich until 20 years ago.

The hills over there were created by filling them with parts of Munich and other areas of Germany damaged during World War II.

View from the Olympiaturm

I hope we spend hours here! Oh no, my humans are leaving the Olympiaturm and getting back on the bus. They're getting off at the train station – are we going home?

Nein (No in German) – they are boarding a train for Berlin, the capital of Germany, and an important place in recent history. Gretta and Hans, can you come with us?

An "ß" is a German letter called Eszett or scharfes. It represents a silent 's' like the second 's' in the word "hiss."

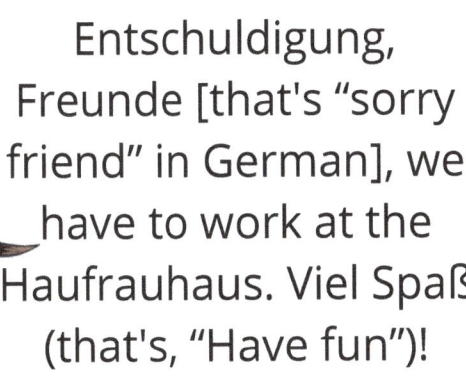

Entschuldigung, Freunde [that's "sorry friend" in German], we have to work at the Haufrauhaus. Viel Spaß (that's, "Have fun")!

28

Hop on the train. This is a high-speed train, and the Germans call it the InterCity Express (ICE). It rockets between cities at 300 km (186 miles) per hour. We're pulling into the **Hauptbahnhof (Berlin Central Station)**, the biggest train station in all of Europe!

Berlin is the largest city in Germany and in the European Union plus it is the capital of Germany. It played a major role during World War II and has more than 170 museums, hundreds of monuments, and many other buildings and places that help tell its story.

Berlin Central Station

My humans are walking toward the **River Spree**, which has flowed through Berlin since it first became a city 800 years ago. When the city was divided, it was a border river between East and West Berlin. As you walk through this area, you see many things honoring people who died during World War II.

After World War II, East Berlin belonged to East Germany— it had many rules and little color. West Berlin was free and full of color. A big wall – called the Berlin Wall (see page 38) — was built in 1961 to keep people in the two Berlins apart. The Wall came down in 1989 and the two Berlins became one again.

Spree River

My humans are walking over to one of the most visited places in the city – the **Reichstag building**.

The Reichstag is Germany's parliament building, and the nation's leaders have met there for many years.

It's easy to spot because of the clear glass dome on the top.

The dome tells the people of Berlin that the government will always be honest with them.

The Reichstag

Now my humans are walking over to **Tiergarten Park** - Berlin's central park. It's huge – 520 acres – and it would take me about 2 hours to rocket around it all. It used to be the hunting grounds for the German prince. It had deer, boar, and other animals. Its name means "animal garden."

Now my humans are heading over to the **Victory Column** in Tiergarten Park.

It was built in honor of a German military victory and has a golden statue on top that represents the Roman goddess of victory, Victoria. Look how shiny she is.

Victory Column

Wait – where are my humans? Walking toward the **Brandenburg Gate (Brandenburger Tor in German),** at the other end of Tiergarten Park and at the end of the beautiful **Unter den Linden (Friedrichstraße** in German) – many celebrations and parades have started or ended here.

It's the last of the original eight stone city gates and a famous Berlin landmark. It was built 150 years ago as a symbol of peace. The Quadriga on the top is a statue of a chariot drawn by four horses.

Brandenburg Gate

Let's have a parade down the grand Unter den Linden Boulevard. Step two! Step two – great job! Wait, where are my humans? They're getting on that bus – hop on!

There's **Bebelplatz,** and over there is the green dome of **St. Hedwig's Cathedral**. Bebelplatz is called the "Empty Library" because book burnings took place here years ago. Book burnings -- yikes!

Over there is the **Deutsches Historisches (History) Museum** – it looks new compared to many of the other old buildings around here.

Deutsches Historisches

Speaking of museums, here's **Museum Island,** an actual island in the middle of Berlin that is home to five incredible museums and **the Berlin Cathedral,** the largest church in the city.

On Museum Island:
- **Bode Museum** – *Byzantine art and coins*
- **Pergamon Museum –** *Pergamon Altar, Ishtar Gate from Babylon*

Museum Island

- ***Alte Nationalgalerie (Old National Gallery)** – Paintings and sculptures from the 1800's*
- ***Neues Museum (New Museum)** -- Egyptian and prehistoric collections*
- ***Altes (Old) Museum** -- Greek and Roman items*

And there's the **Humboldt Forum**, which is part of the **Berlin Palace**, another famous museum. Now we're driving by **St. Mary's Church (Marienkirche)** – the building with the green spires. It was built 800 years ago and it has famous frescos inside, which means art is painted into the walls.

Look, there's the **Rotes Rathaus (Red City Hall)**, where the Governing Mayor and the Berlin Senate work. You can tell this important building by its red brick and clock tower.

Red City Hall

And there's the **Fernsehturm Berlin (Berlin TV Tower)** – the tallest structure in Germany and the third tallest in the European Union.

The tower is 368 meters – or 1,200 feet – tall. It was built by the former East German government in the 1960's.

It sits in the famous **Alexander Platz (Alexander Square)**, and the elevator takes you up to its sphere in a just 40 seconds – rocket speed!

You can see all over Berlin when you're at the top.

Berlin TV Tower

And look – there it is – the **Berlin Wall,** the perfect place to talk about East and West Germany! My humans are getting off.

This is not just any wall – it's a world-famous landmark, art gallery, and memorial.

The Wall was built in 1961 to divide East Berlin and West Berlin.

The Berlin Wall kept friends and even family members apart.

Berlin Wall

It stood for 28 years, as the line between people who were free (on the West side), and people who were not (on the East side). Large sections of the Wall still stand today and colorful art and signs with stories of things that happened here cover parts of it.

With all the history here, this is one of the most interesting places you can visit. Hop on!

Berlin Wall

Checkpoint Charlie

Now we're driving across **Oberbaum Bridge (Oberbaumbrücke)** to go into the southern part of the city. It's a double-decker bridge that crosses the River Spree, has two towers, and used to be a border crossing after World War II.

There's **Checkpoint Charlie** -- the most famous border crossing from former East Berlin to West Berlin. If we step here, we're in what used to be East Berlin, and if we step over here – near the huge American flag, we're in what was West Berlin.

Where did my humans go? Oh, look, they're walking into the **Jewish Museum Berlin**. This is where Jewish neighborhoods used to be but they were destroyed by the Nazis – the government that ran Germany – during World War II.

The Jewish Museum Berlin tells the story of the social, political, and cultural history of the Jewish people in Germany and all over Europe through letters, diaries, and personal items from across 1,000 years.

There's nothing else like it in the world.

Jewish Museum Berlin

I could spend the rest of the day here in the Jewish Museum Berlin, but my humans are getting back on the bus again.

I wonder where we're going now?

We're heading into the western part of the city.

A lot of this area was destroyed or damaged during World War II and had to be rebuilt after the war.

Jewish Museum Berlin

The western part of the city includes:

Potsdamer Platz – a high-tech part of Berlin with really cool architecture.

Gropiusbau – has a museum of applied arts, with art that can be used, like furniture.

KaDeWe – a huge store that has been open for 100 years.

Kurfürstendamm, or "Ku'damm," a two-mile-long street the royal family used to ride their horses down to go into **Grunewald forest**, the largest green space in Berlin.

This might be the best trip ever.

The bus is really moving now. Wait – did that sign say, Flughafen (Airport in English)? Our trip is OVER?!! I'm sad that we're done rocketing around but I am ready for a nap. I love sleeping on airplanes! Well friend, this is where I have to say, Auf Wiedersehen (Goodbye in German), and I will sneak into Emma's backpack and onto the plane.

Thanks for rocketing around with me.

See you on our next adventure!

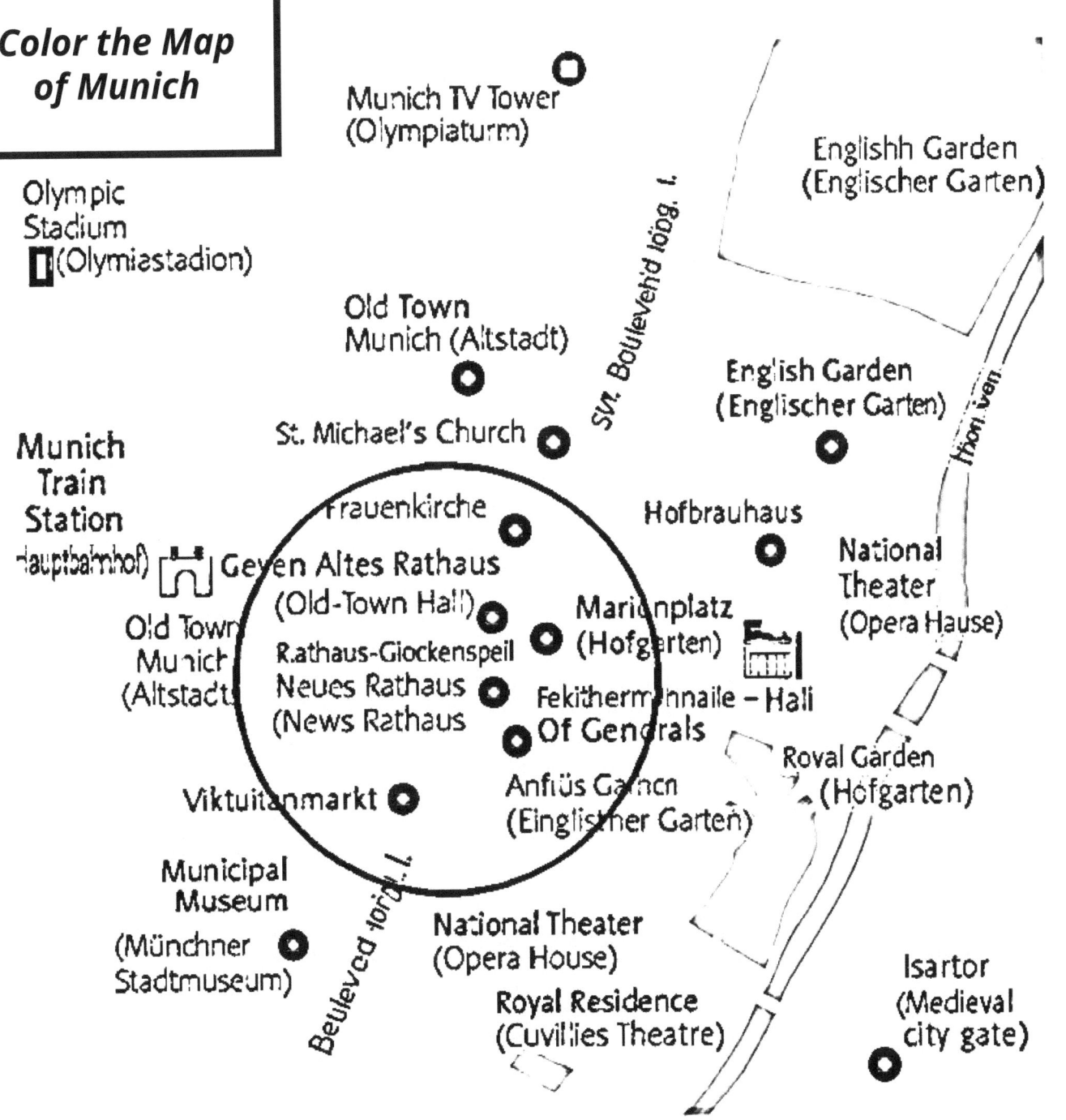

Color the Map of Munich

Munich TV Tower (Olympiaturm)

Englishh Garden (Englischer Garten)

Olympic Stadium (Olymiastadion)

Old Town Munich (Altstadt)

St. Michael's Church

Slr. Boulevend lôbg. l.

English Garden (Englischer Garten)

Thon iven

Munich Train Station (Hauptbahnhof)

Geyen Altes Rathaus (Old-Town Hall)

Frauenkirche

Hofbrauhaus

National Theater (Opera Hause)

Old Town Munich (Altstadt)

R.athaus-Glockenspeil

Neues Rathaus (News Rathaus

Marienplatz (Hofgarten)

Fekitherm hnaile – Hall

Viktuitanmarkt

Of Generals

Anfiüs Garncn (Einglisther Garten)

Roval Garden (Hofgarten)

Municipal Museum (Münchner Stadtmuseum)

Beuleved loròg. l.

National Theater (Opera House)

Royal Residence (Cuvillies Theatre)

Isartor (Medieval city gate)

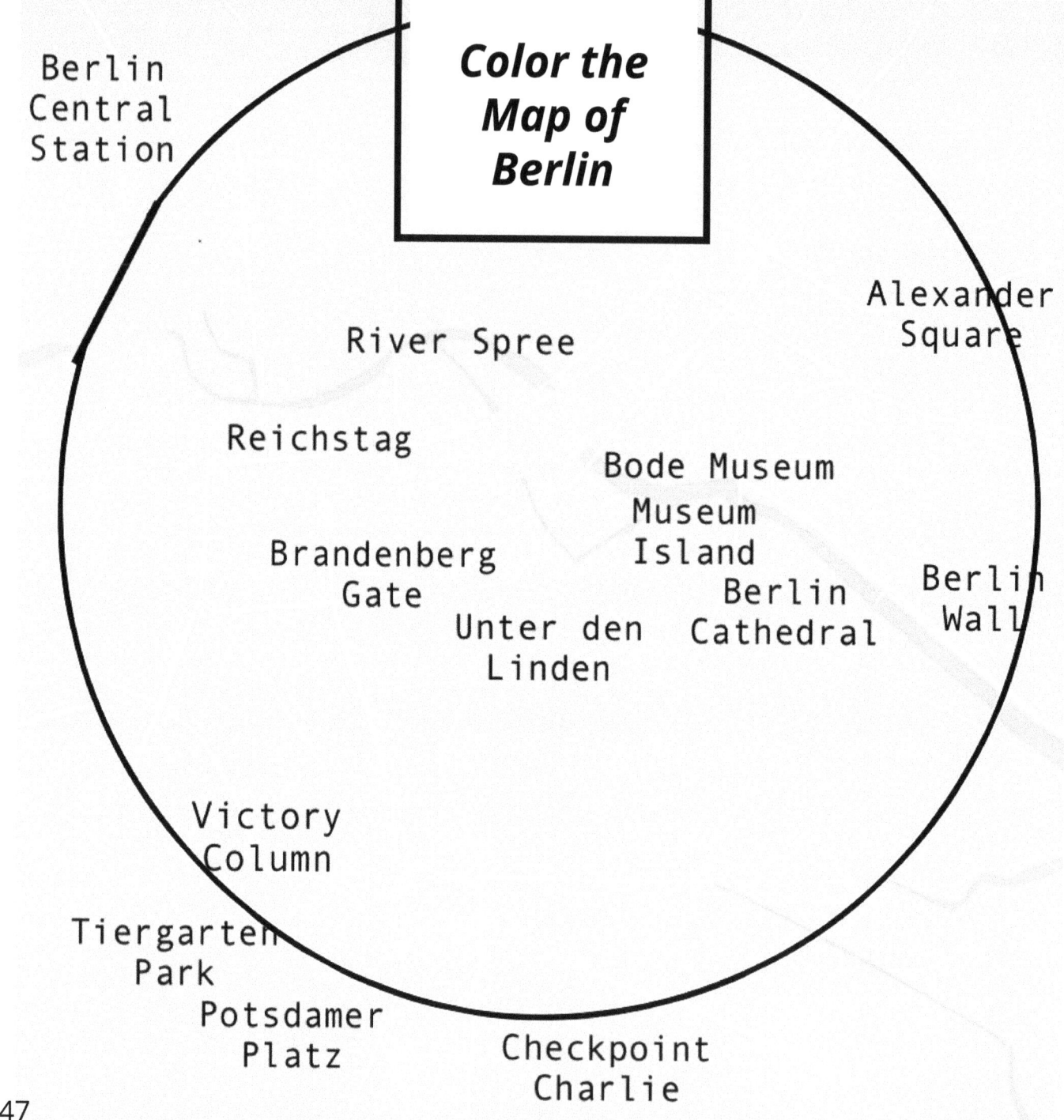

Color the
Map of
Berlin

Berlin
Central
Station

Alexander
Square

River Spree

Reichstag

Bode Museum
Museum
Island

Brandenberg
Gate

Berlin
Cathedral

Berlin
Wall

Unter den
Linden

Victory
Column

Tiergarten
Park

Potsdamer
Platz

Checkpoint
Charlie

German Phrases

German is the national language of Germany.

English	German
Hello	Hallo
How are you today?	Wie geht es dir heute
My name is	Wie heissen Sie
Can you help me	Kannst du mir helfen
Where is	Wo ist
I am lost	Ich bin verloren
I love to rocket around	Ich liebe es, durch die Gegend zu rasen
How do you say in English?	Wie sagst du das auf Englisch
Goodbye!	Auf Wiedersehen!

Other Places to Visit

<u>Munich</u>

-Alter Hof (First ducal residence)
-Asam Church (Asamkirche)
-Isartor (Medieval city gate)
-River Isar
-Sendlinger Tor (Medieval City Gates)
-Theatine Church - St. Kajetan

<u>Berlin</u>

-Berlin Art Market
-Computerspielemuseum (Berlin Computer Games Museum)
-DejaVu Museum
-Deutsches Technikmuseum (Museum of Technology) Features the State -Opera House (Staatsoper Unter den Linden)

Berlin cont.
-Gendarmenmarkt
-Humboldt University
-Kaiser Wilhelm Memorial Church (Gedächtniskirche)
-Lustgarten
-Lützowplatz
-Marie-Elisabeth-Lüders-Haus and River Spree
-Sea Life Berlin
-Sinti and Roma of Europe Murdered under National Socialism Memorial
-Tauentzienstraße
-Templehof
-The DDR Museum
-Zoo / Bikini Berlin

Be a Rocketarounder!

--Read *Rocket Around Germany* AND do activities on rocketaround.com - Join Rocket in building your brain through adventure, imagination, and finding new ways to have fun!

--Let Rocket's human family know: Where should Rocket and his humans go next? Where would your dog want to rocket around with Rocket? (make sure your mom and dad are okay with it first). Email your ideas to lee@rocketaround.com

If you did these things, GREAT JOB! You are an official Rocketarounder... welcome to the Club!

Rocket Around

Germany

I'M A ROCKETAROUNDER!

I build my brain through:

-Adventure

-Imagination

-Finding new ways to have fun!

50

Rocket + The Humans

Rocket is real, and he lives with his neurodiverse human family in Alexandria, VA.

His humans love adventure and traveling, reading, writing, sports, music, chess, anime, drawing, and sleeping.

They hope you enjoyed this book and that you'll read the next one!

More from Rocket Around

Books:

Rocket Around Washington DC – a neurodiverse visual guide with activities
Rocket Around Washington DC – a neurodiverse storybook
Rocket Around Washington DC! Neurodiverse activity + coloring book
Rocket Around Washington DC Ebook
Rocket Around Switzerland - Neurodiverse-friendly visual guide + activities
Rocket Around Switzerland - Neurodiverse-friendly storybook
Rocket Around Switzerland! Neurodiverse-friendly activity + coloring book
Rocket Around Germany - Neurodiverse-friendly storybook
Rocket Around Germany - Neurodiverse-friendly activity + coloring book

On the Internet:

Rocketaround.com *blogsite on adventure & life for neuodiverse families*

Facebook - https://www.facebook.com/groups/rocketaround

Instagram - https://instagram.com/rocketaroundtheglobe?igshid=YmMyMTA2M2Y=)

Pinterest - https://www.pinterest.com/rocketaround/

ISBN: 979-8-9889331-7-5

Look for other Rocket Around books and kids' activities at rocketaround.com!